Photo by Linda Rutenberg

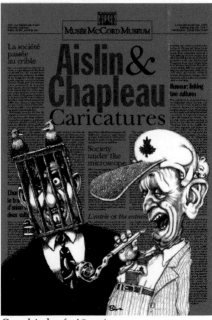

Graphic by épi©entre

AISLIN is the name of Terry Mosher's elder daughter, and the pen-name he uses as the political cartoonist for The Montreal Gazette. Syndicated throughout Canada, Mosher has free-lanced for The New York Times, Time, The National Lampoon, Harper's, The Atlantic Monthly and Punch.

Mosher, 54, was born in Ottawa. He attended 14 different schools in Montreal, Toronto and Quebec City, graduating from the École des Beaux-arts in 1967. He has travelled extensively for The Gazette, writing and drawing interpretive sketchbooks throughout Canada, the U.S., Northern Ireland, Russia, Cuba and North Africa.

The recipient of two National Newspaper Awards and five individual prizes from The International Salon of Caricature, in 1985 Mosher was inducted into The Canadian News Hall of Fame.

Interested in the new technology, Mosher's home page on the Internet, featuring his daily Gazette cartoon, was judged the most entertaining Canadian web site for 1996 (www.montrealgazette.com/AISLIN/).

An avid baseball fan, Mosher is as a 20-year member of The Baseball Writers' Association of America, voting annually for Baseball's Hall of Fame in Cooperstown, N.Y.

Montreal's McCord Museum is presently hosting a large exhibition of caricatures by both AISLIN and SERGE CHAPLEAU, the editorial page cartoonist for La Presse. The exhibit is on display until August, 1998.

Aislin's e-mail address is: aislin@zercom.net

ONE OAR IN THE WATER

The Nasty 90s continued in cartoons by AISLIN

Introduction by Peter Mansbridge

Text by Terry Mosher

Edited by Joe Fiorito

Book design by Mary Hughson

Little, Brown Canada

BOSTON • NEW YORK • TORONTO • LONDON

Copyright © 1997 by Terry Mosher   ISBN # 316-038423
Printed in Canada

Other books by Aislin:
   Aislin–100 Caricatures (1971)
   Hockey Night in Moscow (1972, with Jack Ludwig)
   Aislin–150 Caricatures (1973)
   The Great Hockey Thaw (1974, with Jack Ludwig)
   'Ello, Morgentaler? Aislin–150 Caricatures (1975)
   O.K. Everybody Take a Valium! Aislin–150 Caricatures (1977)
   L'Humour d'Aislin (1977)
   The Retarded Giant (1977, with Bill Mann)
   The Hecklers: A History of Canadian Political Cartooning (1979, with Peter Desbarats)
   The Year The Expos Almost Won the Pennant (1979, with Brodie Snyder)
   Did the Earth Move? Aislin–180 Caricatures (1980)
   The Year The Expos Finally Won Something (1981, with Brodie Snyder)
   The First Great Canadian Trivia Quiz (1981, with Brodie Snyder)
   Stretchmarks (1982)
   The Anglo Guide to Survival in Quebec (1983, with various Montreal writers)
   Tootle: A Children's Story (1984, with Johan Sarrazin)
   Where's the Trough? (1985)
   Old Whores (1987)
   What's the Big Deal? Questions and Answers on Free Trade (1988, with Rick Salutin)
   The Lawn Jockey (1989)
   Parcel of Rogues (1990, with Maude Barlow)
   Barbed Lyres, Canadian Venomous Verse (1990, with various Canadian poets)
   Drawing Bones–15 Years of Cartooning Brian Mulroney (1991)
   Put Up & Shut Up! The 90s so far in Cartoons (1994, with Hubie Bauch)
   Oh, Canadians! Hysterically Historical Rhymes (1986, with Gordon Snell)

Canadian Cataloguing in Publication Data

Aislin
        One oar in the water : the nasty nineties continued
in cartoons

ISBN 0-316-03842-3

1. Canada – Politics and government – 1993-   –
Caricatures and cartoons.*   2. Quebec (Province) –
Politics and government – 1994-   – Caricatures and
cartoons.*   3. Canadian wit and humor, Pictorial.
I. Title.

NC1449.A37A4 1997   971.064'8'0207   C97-931669-3

10 9 8 7 6 5 4 3 2 1

LITTLE, BROWN AND COMPANY (CANADA) LIMITED
148 YORKVILLE AVENUE,
TORONTO, ON, CANADA, M5R 1C2

CONTENTS

INTRODUCTION

"Did you see Aislin this morning?"

Those six words bring fear to the hearts of most public figures in Canada. Immediately they assume they've become the target of one of the most deft pens in the country. That something they've done, or perceived to have done, is now being held up to national ridicule, embarrassment or derision – or worse, all of the above.

I know. I've been there. And it's quite a journey. I remember the first time. Initially, when a friend asked me that dreaded six word question, I swelled with a strange sense of having "made it." But it was a brief feeling. One glance at my friend's face and I realized it wasn't envy I was looking at, but sympathy. The rest of the day was spent trying not to notice the snickers on my colleague's faces as I moved around the newsroom.

But of course, there's more to Terry Mosher's editorial artwork than skewering the skewerable. A lot more. In the business of Canadian journalism few, if any, can capture the moment – whether it's one of angst, pride, sorrow or happiness – better. In the second of his 90s trilogy, he captures all of them.

Sit back. Relax. And start turning the pages. And oh yes, if you are one of those who suddenly see yourself staring back from one of these pages, feel honoured. Somehow.

Peter Mansbridge
Lac St Germain, Québec
August 1997

THANKS

Special thanks to Gaëtan Côté, my main man at The Gazette.
Also to Todd Bedbrook, Dominique Jaune, Pat Duggan,
Dave Stubbs, Don Macpherson and Henry Aubin for
various and sundry.

OTTAWA

WELL, MR. PRESIDENT, OTTAWA'S SMALLER THAN WASHINGTON BUT ABOUT THE SAME SIZE AS LITTLE ROCK—AND JUST AS INCESTUOUS...

U.S. President Bill Clinton visits Ottawa for the first time

Now that he has served one term as Prime Minister, how does Jean Chrétien compare to his predecessor, Brian Mulroney? (We're excluding Kim Campbell here; she was but a blip on the screen.)

Chrétien is enjoying an unprecedented honeymoon with the Canadian public, probably because by the time he resigned, Brian Mulroney was the most unpopular Prime Minister in Canadian history.

Having endured Mulroney's arrogant flamboyance, honeyed drawl and Gucci shoes, Canadians were eager to put their faith in a little guy from Shawinigan.

Mulroney's government spent money like drunken sailors – Liberal drunken sailors. Chrétien's first term was characterized by a sour, fiscally conservative scent. Or perhaps that's just the odour of the $40 billion deficit left behind by the Tories.

Any hopes Mulroney may have had of being remembered fondly in the history books were dashed with the 1994 publication of Stevie Cameron's *On The Take: Crime, Corruption and Greed in the Mulroney Years.* The book was a litany of sins committed by many of Mulroney's cronies during his two terms in power.

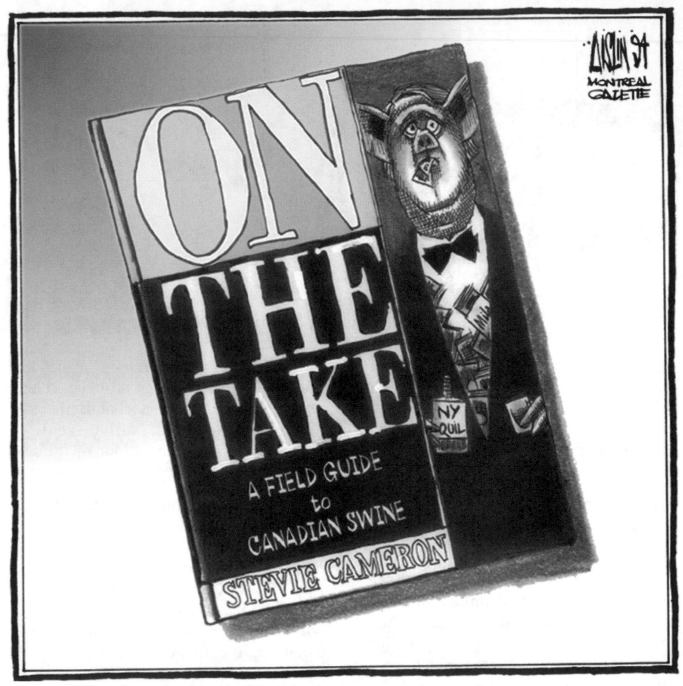

ON THE TAKE – a devastating chronicle of the Mulroney years

Cameron, however, admitted that she still couldn't find the "smoking gun"; she was unable to prove a widespread rumour that Mulroney had been paid several million dollars by anonymous donors to quit.

No matter; after leaving office, Mulroney swiftly took advantage of contacts made while Prime Minister to travel the world doing business, making himself even more wealthy.

Alas, while he may be welcome in the financial palaces of the world, Mulroney rarely shows his face in Montreal. The former Prime Minister used to walk his dog in a Westmount park until he was told by a fellow dog-fancier that he should scoop his dog's poop. Mulroney would not stoop, and hasn't been seen walking the poodle since.

In addition to the deficit, the Liberals inherited the GST, which they ran against but left in place; they also inherited the Free Trade Agreement, which they had run against in 1988, but left in place.

Free trade is either the "greatest" or the "worst" thing to have happened to us, depending on which talking head is doing the talking, or whose figures catch your fancy.

The Mulroney legacy: A $40 billion deficit

Canadian reaction to the Helms-Burton Act

Let Jesse Helms kiss our butts!

Canada Hand to be added to the Canadarm

But the Americans continue their habit of pushing us around when it suits them. Witness Senator Jesse Helms, chairman of the U.S. Senate Foreign Relations Committee, who managed to pass the Helms-Burton Act, a scrap of legislation denying entry to the U.S. to anyone who benefits from American property confiscated by Castro. This has had the grand effect of keeping one or two Canadians out of the U.S., and prompted some loud beating-of-the-drum by Canadian nationalists.

Despite these occasional glitches, Canadians seem quite happy to cozy up to the Americans, as long as we can hitch a ride on their coattails. Canadian astronauts soar into the heavens aboard U.S. rockets for the proud privilege of operating the Canadarm. Now we're investing $207 million in something to attach to it: the Canada Hand.

No pun intended, but the Liberals originally maintained there should be more of an arm's length relationship between our country and the U.S., given Brian Mulroney's habit of vacationing with American Presidents. Nevertheless, Jean Chrétien is just as anxious as Mulroney to buddy up to the Oval Office; he's formed a tight bond with fellow golfer Bill Clinton.

Jean Chrétien visits the White House

Break-in at 24 Sussex Drive

That's Bill Clinton, not Bill Clennett.

When the RCMP hired the Disney Corporation to market their souvenirs, it all seemed a bit much. And our poor redcoats never looked so Goofy as they did the night they fell asleep at the post, allowing an intruder to break into 24 Sussex Drive.

The culprit was fended off by Aline Chrétien, armed with an Eskimo sculpture. This may explain the Prime Minister's zeal in wringing the neck of demonstrator Bill Clennett several months later. We trust the PM's male ego has been restored.

"I took him out!"

14

PRIME MINISTER · PREMIER MINISTRE

October 29, 1994

A CONFIDENTIAL LETTER TO
ALL MY CABINET MINISTERS

All my Cabinet Ministers:

This will be my first—and last—letter to you idiots.

For decades, I was a successful Cabinet Minister who never got into any trouble, primarily because I never wrote any letters; I used the telephone instead.

From now on, none of you are to write any letters whatsoever. Henceforth, use the telephone (but never cellulars!).

X

Anonymous

P.S. This letter will self-destruct (as you will if it goes unheeded).

Government leaks

15

Chrétien and Bouchard hold a mutual press conference

Chrétien depends on a loyal staff to keep him, whenever possible, out of harm's way. No great intellect (a hindrance in politics at times), Chrétien relies on those closest to him to get things done. Any show of dissent within the governing Liberal caucus is severely dealt with while the PM and his advisors get on with the business of running Canada, or at the very least, trying to keep it together.

Inevitably, some cracks have begun to appear in Jean Chrétien's visage. During a nationally televised town hall meeting, for which he was clearly unprepared, Chrétien lied and claimed he had never, ever, promised to eliminate the GST. (Sheila Copps had already been through the muck on this one; having promised to resign if the GST wasn't eliminated, she finally did so [under extreme media pressure] only to be immediately re-elected in a by-election.)

Lying in politics – a necessity for anyone who wants to get elected – is part of the game; the trick is not to get caught, particularly on national TV.

The Prime Minister eventually apologized, and the country forgave him enough to re-elect his government. Or maybe the country simply decided Chrétien was the lesser of all other evils.

Chrétien apologizes for televised town hall remarks

Walt Disney Corporation to market RCMP's souvenirs

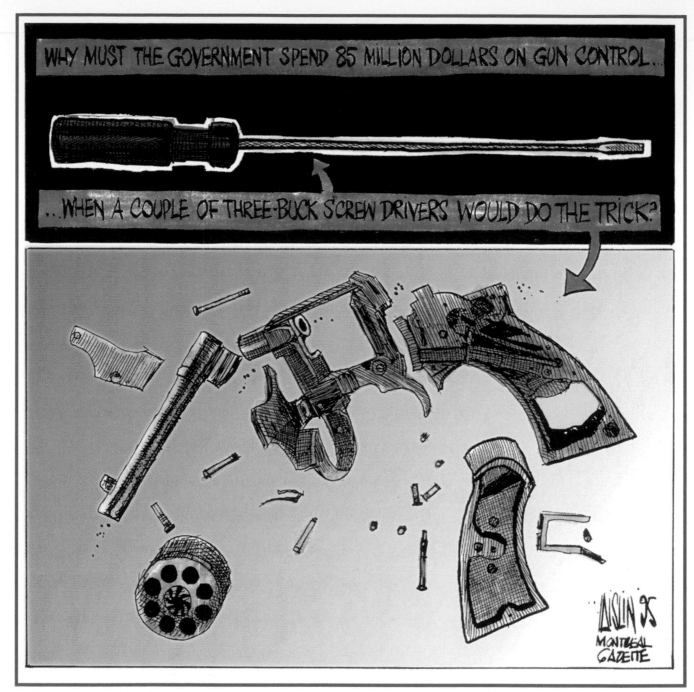

Modest gun control legislation introduced

Are we headed for a two-tiered medicare system?

Sheila Copps, who had promised to quit if the GST wasn't eliminated, finally did

MICHEL GAUTHIER *
*MONSIEUR FOOTNOTE

Unknown Leader of the Opposition, Michel Gauthier

WHEN PRESTON MANNING VISITS QUÉBEC, REMEMBER THAT TWO NEGATIVES DON'T MAKE A POSITIVE...

NON!

Preston Manning visits Quebec during the Referendum

Despite the presence of four alternative political parties, Canada seems bent on choosing its leadership from the Liberals. What choice do we have? After the annihilation of the Tories in 1993, the resulting void in the House of Commons was filled by two rump parties: the separatist Bloc Québécois, and the Reform Party from the West.

The rumps are of roughly equal size.

The Bloc was led by its founder, Lucien Bouchard, until he decided to go home, and lead the Parti Québécois. The Bloc then chose Michel Gauthier to be its new leader, and by default, Canada's new Leader of the Opposition. Speaking little English, Gauthier arrived on the federal scene a virtual nobody; he departed the same way, and was replaced by the hapless Gilles Duceppe just in time for the 1997 federal election.

Reform leader Preston Manning, who speaks no French, is popular in the West. However, his party is looked upon with suspicion anywhere east of the Manitoba border. For some reason, Reform attracts more than its share of political wing-nuts. Manning himself has acquaintances in far-right circles south of the border, and to

Newfoundland feuds with Quebec over Churchill Falls power prices

many Canadians he seems a kind of northern Ross Perot – a man who tilts a bit too far off-centre.

Consequently, neither the BQ nor Reform has a snowball's chance of ever forming a government, unless traditional old Ontario rejects the Liberals and votes Reform – a highly unlikely scenario. This seems to guarantee that the Liberals will remain in power until one of two events occurs: the re-emergence of the Tories as a national party, or the separation of Quebec.

There have been some notable heroics in the Canadian political arena over the last three years. On both coasts, Newfoundland and British Columbia happily stood up to foreign powers – over fish, of all things.

Brian Tobin, formerly the Federal Minister of Fisheries and Oceans, returned to Newfoundland to become Premier. Happy on home ground, Tobin immediately began waving the flag in response to Spanish overfishing of our already-depleted turbot stocks. Canada seized a Spanish trawler; there were massive anti-Canadian demonstrations in Spain.

And then the mighty Tobin went after Lucien Bouchard, demanding more money for the cheap power sent to Quebec from Churchill Falls in Labrador.

Newfoundland takes on the Spanish

British Columbia takes on the Yanks

Fish wars

Anti-Canadian demonstrations held in Spain

East coast fish

West coast fish

Recognizing a good tactic when he saw one, Glen Clark, the newly elected NDP Premier of British Columbia, went toe-to-toe with the Americans, in response to Yankee overfishing of Canadian salmon on the west coast.

Meanwhile, back in Ottawa, the Liberals simply went about their business, trying not to get involved, and doing a brisk and bland job of eliminating most of the deficit. Indeed, with all the hoopla surrounding the various Team Canada trade missions, you'd think everything was rosy in the Great White North. It's not.

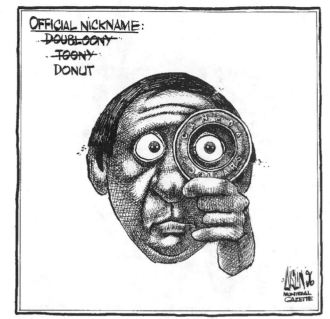

New $2 coins are popping apart

Team Canada pursues business in Asia

Banff threatened by over-tourism

Military hazing videos surface

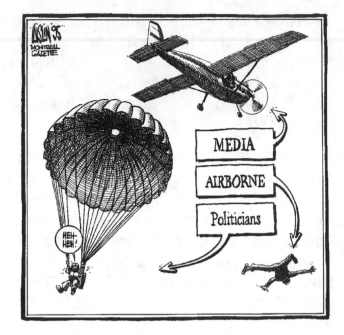

The economy is still sluggish, and there are still too many people without work. But at least we're still good at something – a recent UN study on the environment rated Canada one of the world's worst polluters. Oh, and we're great vacationers – the jewel of our national parks system, Banff, is now in danger of being overrun by tourists.

There was a bit of comic relief when the two-dollar Polar Bear coin was introduced; easily amused bar-room wits had great fun popping out the centres.

The worst scandal to erupt during Chrétien's first term was not even one of the Liberal's own making – there were strange goings-on during a Canadian peacekeeping mission to Somalia in 1993, while the Tories were still in power.

A Somali teenager was captured and tortured to death by Canadian Airborne troops; the young man's brutalization was vividly photographed by his assailants.

Further, videotapes of violent hazing ceremonies began to surface, landing in the lap of Defence Minister David Collenette who eventually had to step down. The once-proud Airborne was disbanded.

This led to the establishment of an extensive and expensive government

Military red tape

inquiry into the activities of the Canadian military in Somalia, and a seemingly endless parade of top brass ducking for cover on national television every night.

This shameful display led to the Somalia Inquiry's most damning charge, that there had been a cover-up. Liberal politicians, including the Prime Minister, denied there had been any cover-up, and forced the Somalia Inquiry to wrap up their investigation.

Subsequently, the effectiveness – and, indeed, the usefulness – of all government inquiries is now being seriously questioned.

Despite Somalia Inquiry report, PM denies any cover-up

ANNOUNCING THE LATEST AWARD-OF-MERIT MEDAL, THE *BULL SHOOTER*, TO BE PRESENTED BY ART EGGLETON TO SENIOR MEMBERS OF THE ARMED FORCES WHO MANAGED TO PAPER-SHRED THEIR WAY THROUGH THE RECENT SOMALIA INQUIRY

Politically corrected

Sixty percent of Canadians no longer think of themselves as either right or left. Politics, as we've understood them in the past, are dying. After the fall of Communism, for a brief moment it seemed there might be a new utopia, with the sound of freedom ringing throughout the world.

Why, then, is life so much nastier than it was even 10 years ago? Perhaps because the new world order is not about freedom, it's about monopoly capitalism. We live in a world where the gap between rich and poor is growing, and where we cynically understand that justice is wholly dependent on the size of our wallet.

We can't hide at home because we are hooked to our televisions, our radios, our telephones, and now to our computers. The media keep us informed, all right; informed about what we should buy.

Real news is, of course, still available. But more and more, it's becoming harder to tell the difference between news, gossip and disaster. Welcome to the wonderful world of infotainment. We read about the killing of fashion designer Gianni Versace in the New York Times; and then we

Astrologist Jo-Jo Savard's company goes bankrupt

Sea-Doo accident kills two small children

See-through fashions featured in a February Gazette

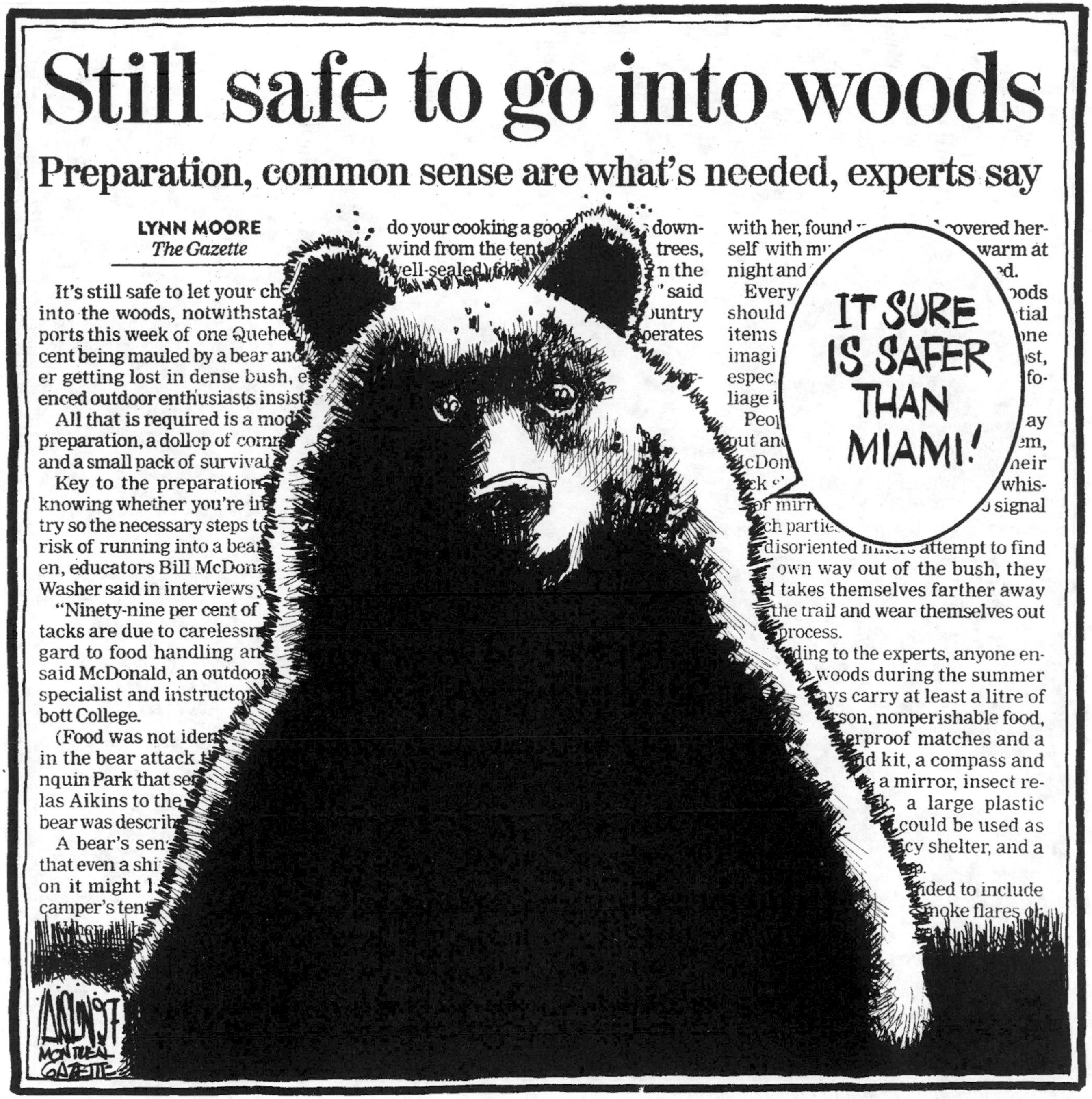

Fashion designer Versace murdered in Miami

Shocking Oklahoma bombing kills 168 people

watched the killer pursued on *Entertainment Tonight*.

Therapy seems to be today's growth industry, but for those who can't afford it, the world is full of quack astrologers and talk shows aiming to help us cope with the dysfunction-of-the-day.

And then there are those self-sufficient souls who try to change the world by taking matters into their own hands. Like the Unabomber. Like the paramilitary rat who blew up the Federal Building in Oklahoma. And like the countless gun-toting paranoids holed up in the back woods of America with their conspiracy theories, their dynamite and their automatic weapons.

It makes us pine for the simpler days of student demonstrations, when there was the faint smell of flags burning in the air and the protests were against the injustice of real, and not imaginary, wars.

And then there was O.J. The whole world was hooked on the TV coverage of the trial of this black sports hero/B-grade movie actor accused of the brutal murder of his white wife and her lover.

Innocent or guilty, it didn't matter; we all found ourselves polarized along the nasty

Right-wing militias abound in the U.S.

TWA crash kills 230 – reasons unknown

Wednesday 7PM 9PM

7PM ② **CBS NEWS (CC)** — Chung/Rather
The O.J. Simpson trial, continued.
② **NBC NEWS (CC)** — Tom Brokaw
The O.J. Simpson trial, continued.
③ **ABC NEWS (CC)** — Peter Jennings
The O.J. Simpson trial, continued.
④⑤ **THE SIMPSONS (CC)**
Homer and Bart Simpson watch the ongoing
O.J. Simpson trial. A barrel of laughs!
⑥⑦ **ENTERTAINMENT TONIGHT (CC)**
Exclusive footage of O.J. Simpson, killing time
in his cell, watching reruns of The Simpsons.
⑧ **MacNEIL, LEHRER (CC) 1:00**
A panel discussion on the moral influence that
the U.S.—the only remaining superpower—has
on the rest of the world.

lines of race and class. No matter what you think of the verdict, this much remains true in the United States: you can buy justice. And if you watched the trial, you know bullshit still baffles brains.

We Canadians tut-tutted.

After all, our system of justice is far superior, our media are much more pure, and we certainly don't go in for that kind of public spectacle up here, no sir, not us. And then came Paul Bernardo. We did not tut-tut.

We gagged – and kept watching...

THE LATEST 12-STEP GROUP...

...AND I'M POWERLESS OVER LIVE COVERAGE OF THE O.J. TRIAL...

BACK ON THE STREET?...

HI, BABE!

O.J. Simpson found not guilty

BERNARDO!

The Toronto Premiere

Brought to you by:

THE TORONTO STAR   Toronto SUN   CTV

AISLIN '95
MONTREAL GAZETTE

The Middle East continued

Northern Ireland continued

LONDON (Reuter) — An anti-depressant drug makes some patients have an orgasm when they yawn, scientists have discovered.

Republican convention

When those who report the news do their jobs properly, we ought to be able to read the paper or watch TV and come away with an understanding of why the world works the way it does.

And so we watched the Republicans nominate Bob Dole to run for president against Bill Clinton in the 1996 U.S. presidential election. Immediately we were aware of the absence of blacks and other minorities within the GOP.

We listened to Dole trumpet the virtues of old-fashioned family values, knowing he hadn't paid child support after the breakup of his first marriage. And then we saw him stumble, literally and figuratively, from the podium.

But how long can journalists be trusted to retain their impartiality when the media they work for are increasingly subject to monopoly control? How do you evaluate what you hear on the news, knowing that Peter Jennings, the Canadian-born ABC-TV news anchor, works for a company owned by the Disney Corporation?

Canadians take pride in the CBC, one of the best public broadcasters in the world. The CBC's reputation as a newsgatherer is

Walt Disney Corporation buys ABC TV

Deep budget cuts at the CBC

Two editors quit over Conrad Black controlling Southam

the envy of the free world. But we worry that the deep and ongoing cuts, blithely carried out by that mild beancounter Perrin Beatty and his minions, will compromise CBC's quality in the long run.

As for private broadcasters, the plain truth is that the media have to make money to survive. Freedom of the press is guaranteed only to the man who owns one. Conrad Black, an opinionated man, owns more Canadian newspapers than anyone else in the country. His purchase of the Southam newspaper chain led to the resignation of several highly competent, but liberal, editors.

Money talks.

And, in the 1990s, business walks. Those companies that cannot or will not pay attention to globalization will falter. Eaton's, for example, that venerable Canadian institution, is on the verge of bankruptcy because it has yet to figure out a way to compete with American giants like K-mart. CP Air will fall from the sky unless, like Air Canada, it buddies up to larger international airlines.

That other grand old institution, Bell Canada, seems to be hanging on in spite of deregulation, and cutthroat competition.

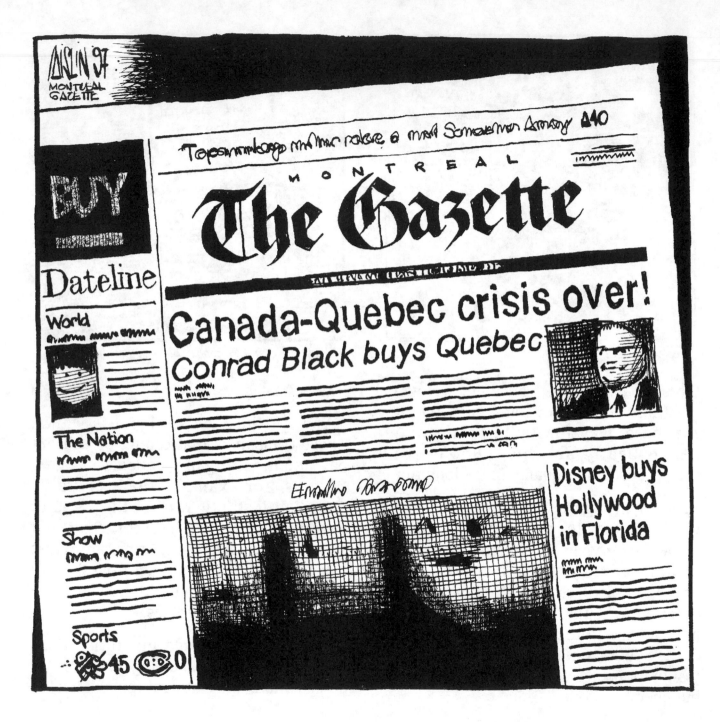

Canadian Airlines in trouble

Bell's solution?

Massive layoffs.

How 90s.

And if you can look at your phone bill and tell me how much money you've saved this month, and if you know just what rate those savings are compared to, then you are a better person than most of the rest of us.

Fortunately, some things do not change. The lure of the fast buck, for one. And how much Bre-X did you own? Oh, well; at least they made their money the old-

Bre-X in trouble

Eaton's in trouble

THIS IS A hOldUP!
GIVe uS YOuR mOneY.
YOu HAVe NO ChOice!

Have A Nice Day,
Your Local Bank

LaPin 95
MONTREAL GAZETTE

Banks record historic profits

fashioned way. They salted the samples.

But if anyone has a licence to print money, it's the banks, all of which seem to survive wonderfully well by doing nothing more complex than manipulating us and our money, and charging us for the privilege.

The biggest threat we face is not the banks, however; not the Internet, not even our own greedy selves. We are blinded by science.

We can clone sheep. What's next?

No, who's next?

Internet Anonymous?

BIRTHS

DEATHS

CLONES

AISLIN 97
MONTREAL
GAZETTE

51

Lucien Bouchard

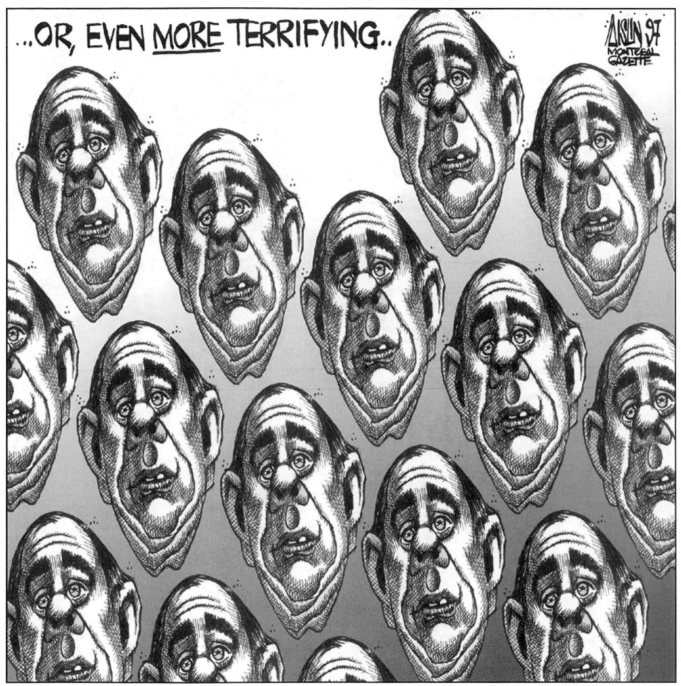

Daniel Johnson

Robert Bourassa: 1933–1996

QUÉBEC

O.K. EVERYBODY TAKE A VALIUM!

Original cartoon drawn when the PQ was first elected in 1976

Robert Bourassa died of melanoma on October 2, 1996. His death marked the end of an era in Quebec politics.

For 30 years, Bourassa made a career of maddening separatists and federalists alike; depending on your point of view, he was either a fence sitter or a tightrope walker.

Above all, he was a master strategist who never met a fixed position he liked. He liked wiggle-room. In the end, Quebeckers took a fixed position of their own; we decided he was one of us.

Politics in Quebec have always been driven by personality. Polls consistently show that 70% of Quebeckers prefer to remain in Canada, provided there is some sort of guarantee of a certain amount of autonomy.

No one has ever been able to come up with a deal that is acceptable, never mind comprehensible (70% of Quebeckers opposed Meech Lake; 82% didn't even understand it).

And so we elect leaders whose destiny is sometimes to build fences, and sometimes to sit on them.

Recently, two dominant personalities have emerged in Quebec politics: Jacques Parizeau and Lucien Bouchard. One is a

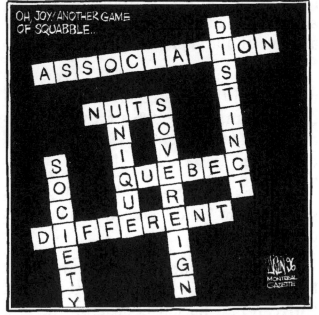

stern pragmatist, the other an arch triumphalist. Typically, neither man can stand the other.

The Soviet Union may have collapsed, South Africa may have cleansed itself of apartheid, there have been genuine attempts at peace in Ireland and the Middle East; in spite of the best efforts of our brightest thinkers, the status of Quebec in Canada still has not been resolved.

Don't hold your breath.

Parizeau is that rare creature, a Quebec nationalist who affects the mannerisms, speech patterns and bespoke tailoring of an English country squire.

A shrewd economist, he has been an important presence within the Parti Québécois since its founding. He was Finance Minister during the Lévesque era, but he quit the party in a huff when he felt Lévesque had gone soft on sovereignty.

After the failures of both Meech Lake and Charlottetown, Quebec nationalists were in a feisty mood. Daniel Johnson, a politician possessing none of Robert Bourassa's strategic brilliance, took over the leadership of the Quebec Liberal Party. Parizeau beat him handily, and was elected Premier on September 12, 1994.

Jacques Parizeau elected as Premier of Quebec

Lisette Lapointe-Parizeau assumes power

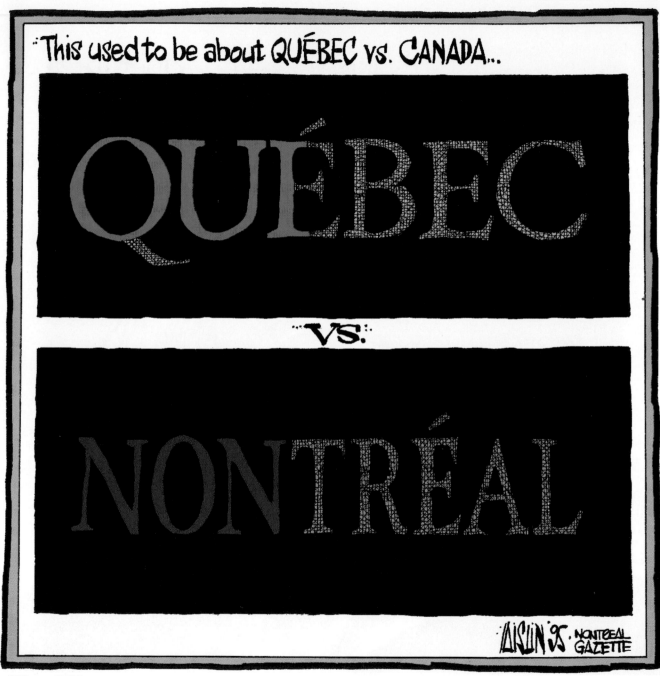

OUIs vs. NONs

Parizeau says that if Quebeckers vote OUI, they'll be cooked just like lobsters

Imagining Canada without Quebec…or Quebec without Canada

Parizeau gives the U.S. some marching orders

"A never ending visit to the dentist." Parizeau

Parizeau gives orders to the rest of Canada

Unfortunately for cartoonists, Parizeau's reign would be a short one.

Having promised to hold a referendum on separation within a year of the election, he set about to do just that. After installing a hardline cabinet, he read the signs and portents and called for a referendum to be held on October 30, 1995 (the day before Hallowe'en).

For a man of his word, Parizeau has trouble keeping his mouth shut, and free of feet. After he was elected, Parizeau trumpeted that the Free Trade Agreement would be kept in place in a separate Quebec (as if, somehow, the Americans would have no say in the matter).

Although the 1995 referendum was one of the most exciting events in Canadian political history, the lead-up to the campaign was utterly flat. Quebeckers traditionally take a long summer vacation from politics of any sort.

The separatist campaign began to look like it would remain stalled. Parizeau himself was the problem – he scares soft sovereigntists and federalists alike.

He tried to smooth his image by publicly signing a document offering Canada an economic and political association with

The OUI side comes up with a series of clever posters

News item: Mario Dumont objects to Liberals calling him a "little asshole" in the National Assembly...

WHY NOT "BIG" LIKE JACQUES PARIZEAU OR LUCIEN BOUCHARD?

TEAM ARROGANCE 0
3ième PERIODE
QQM

Quebec after separation.

Included in the signing ceremony were Lucien Bouchard and Mario Dumont, quasi-separatist and leader of the Action Democratique. (Young Dumont assured himself an eternal place in the history of Quebec politics the day he stood up in the National Assembly and asked that the opposition Liberals stop referring to him as a "little asshole.")

Although Parizeau was elected in part because Quebeckers were angry over the failures of Meech and Charlottetown, the simple fact is that he is not and has never been popular, except perhaps among extreme hardliners.

The pleasure he takes at the table is too great, and he enjoys the finer things in life with a gusto too obvious by half – altogether the wrong image in a province wracked by poverty and unemployment.

Once, in a PQ ad campaign intended to sweeten his image and portray him as a regular guy, Parizeau was shown walking in the woods with a dog. Parizeau doesn't own a dog.

He married longtime member of the PQ, Lisette Lapointe – another devotee of the good life – and quickly appointed his

Jacques and Lisette are sent to the back of the bus

The village priest comes home

blushing bride to a position of power. Lapointe's private life has long been the subject of gossip among the nabobs of Outremont; over the years, she was rumoured to have had a series of affairs with prominent Péquistes. Her appointment was not popular, especially in conservative, rural Quebec.

Parizeau was in trouble early in the campaign, with one poll showing that support for the OUI side had fallen to 38%. Ever the pragmatist, Parizeau swallowed his considerable pride and stepped aside for the sake of the cause, allowing the far more popular Lucien Bouchard to play a leading role during the crucial last three weeks of the campaign.

Bouchard possesses a mystic popularity in Quebec. He is at once a father figure and a village priest whose dark eyes burn with the intensity of Rocket Richard's.

He was also at one time a Mulroney Conservative. Brian appointed him to the Cliche Commission, made him a member of the Tory Cabinet, and sent him to France as our Ambassador. But Bouchard turned his back on Canada after Meech, and created his own party, the Federal separatist Bloc Québécois.

Bouchard refers to Quebec as being a white race

The post-Referendum cartoon...

and the unpublished backup cartoon

Bouchard's shifting political allegiances – he was an admirer of Pierre Trudeau – may infuriate people in the rest of Canada who do not understand Quebec. But here in La Belle Province, changing sides frequently doesn't seem to matter much, as long as you are seen to have the interests of Quebec at heart.

This strategy has worked well for other Quebec politicians, notably Claude Wagner and René Lévesque; so far, it hasn't worked quite so well for Guy Bertrand.

Bouchard's presence at the head of the sovereignty campaign whipped the troops into shape and excited the population. Standing firm on sovereignty while at the same time appealing to softliners, Bouchard insisted he could make a deal with Canada.

Even so, he was – à la Parizeau – not immune to the occasional gaffe. Musing during the campaign on Quebec's low birth rate, he said "We're one of the white races that has the fewest children." This elicited a firestorm of accusations of sexism and racism, especially from Quebec's ethnic population, which has never warmed to the idea of sovereignty.

Parizeau quits after unfortunate money-ethnic remarks

Nevertheless, momentum for the OUI side built steadily. At the last minute, the hitherto complacent federalist forces panicked and called for a giant rally to be held in Montreal on the last weekend of the campaign.

Whether this helped or hurt the cause is a matter of debate. The final results were 50.58% NON, 49.42% OUI. Lobsters across the province breathed a sigh of relief, although Aislin had a backup cartoon ready, in case the vote had gone the other way.

In a bitter Referendum night speech, apparently made while under the influence of something stronger than water, Parizeau blamed the loss on "money and the ethnic vote." He was forced to resign shortly thereafter, because of the unsuitability of his remarks.

No Quebecker likes a sore loser.

And so the road was cleared for Lucien Bouchard to resign as leader of the BQ in Ottawa, and return to Quebec as the crown prince of sovereignty, replacing Parizeau as both head of the Parti Québécois and Premier of Quebec.

For the first time in his life, Lucien Bouchard would actually have to govern.

Unpublished

73

Hospital closings

As he would soon discover, this is not an easy job at the best of times in Quebec.

Sovereignty must appear as the PQ's ultimate goal; at the same time, the Parti Québécois has to maintain an image of fiscal responsibility in an ever-expanding global economy. This can create enormous headaches.

Quebec Premiers are always ready, at the drop of a hat or a writ, to trot off to Wall Street in order to prop up the province's credit rating.

At the same time, the PQ never stops trying to reassure voters that Quebec's lagging economy has nothing at all to do with the political situation.

Yes, well, you try thinking two conflicting and contradictory thoughts at the same time. It's a task which isn't getting any easier.

The PQ was elected on a promise of social democracy. It has delivered a cold-hearted, right-wing agenda of cuts to social programs. Not surprisingly, Bouchard has had battles with Quebec's militant unions, who have threatened to withdraw their traditional, and considerable, support.

A reluctant Team Canada member on a business trip to Asia

Having promised a kind of rapprochement with Quebec anglos, the PQ seems to have used a particularly heavy hand when it comes to closing English hospitals.

But governments are elected to govern, and Bouchard's has adopted the fashionable mania for balanced budgets. He has promised to eliminate the deficit by the turn of the century. Bouchard is, after all, a conservative at heart – remember, he was Brian's pal.

Economic reality dictates that Bouchard must be realistic where Parizeau was cavalier in his dealings with the rest of Canada; and so he tagged along with the rest of the Premiers and business leaders from across the country on the Team Canada trade mission to Asia.

What choice did he have?

Bouchard's rock-solid reputation as the saviour of Quebec could suffer as a result of the economic choices he's had to make. Still, his opponent, Daniel Johnson, is widely seen as a feeble politician, lacking spark and skill.

Johnson is the master of the low profile. Should he win the next provincial election, the question of a third referendum will be

SSJB issues orders on garb allowed in its parade

Raymond Villeneuve of the MLNQ

Published unpublishable cartoon

redundant. That could be his trump card.

If Johnson loses, however, he'll be toast, the game will still be on, and the provincial Liberals will need a new leader, someone capable of taking on Lucien Bouchard in the next election.

Jean Charest, anyone?

As if he didn't have enough on his plate, Bouchard has to deal with the quacks and crazies of the sovereignty movement. They are an embarrassment. One zealot hardliner said he'd ignore any STOP sign with English on it; Aislin wished him well.

The Gazette killed the cartoon, but as a result of a glitch in some new technology, the cartoon made the paper anyway. Several editors suffered heart palpitations that morning. (An internal investigation continues.)

Meanwhile, the Société St. Jean Baptiste has done little to endear itself to the ethnic community, insisting that national costumes are verboten; only pur laine costumes may be worn during the Société's annual parade.

And then there is Raymond Villeneuve, xenophobic former member of the FLQ. His new outfit is Le Mouvement de Libération Nationale du Quebec. On behalf of the MLNQ, Villeneuve opined that violence might be necessary to free Quebec, and that "Jews would be the first to pay for obstructing Quebec's ascension to independence."

Bouchard's troubles do not end here.

Quebec's aboriginal people have grievances of long standing against the provincial government over their rights, over the government's obligations, over the James Bay Hydro project.

And then there are those militant anglos...

Native people won't go

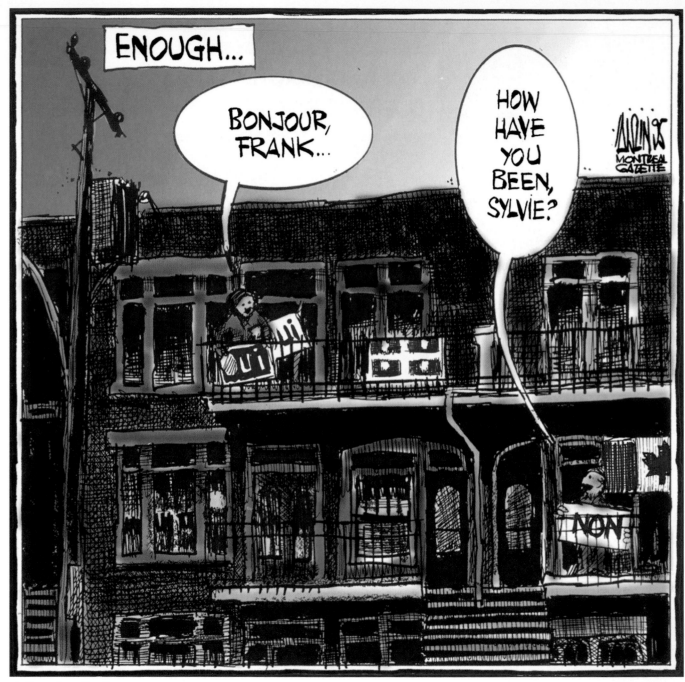

Referendum finally over

Anglophile, Jacques Parizeau

ANGLOS

INTRODUCING INSPECTOR CLOUSEAU OF THE...

OLF

...l'Office de la Langue Française

On October 27, three days before the Quebec Referendum, and in response to polls suggesting the dreaded OUI side just might win, federalists from across the country were urged to flood the streets of downtown Montreal in the hope of convincing Quebeckers to stay in Canada.

Canadians did indeed come from all parts of the country to show their love for Quebec – about 15,000 of them. The other 100,000 spectators and participants were curious Montrealers – plenty of them federalists, many of them anglophones, and some merely folks who love a crowd.

But it was a rare event, if only because Quebec's anglos are not demonstrative by nature. Although they've grumbled about things over the years, the anglophone and ethnic populations that remain in Quebec are far more bilingual than they used to be. And they certainly all know how to read French, given that virtually all public signage in Quebec is now in one language only.

Calm though anglos may be, when it came to the closeness of the referendum, Parizeau's subsequent crack about "money and the ethnic vote," and evidence that there had been widespread vote-tampering in several federalist polls, anglos freaked.

Suddenly, an idea took hold: If Canada could be partitioned, then so could Quebec.

Suddenly, an idea that had previously only been discussed behind closed doors in whispers began to be debated openly.

Quebec's Cree and Inuit populations held their own referendums, voting 94% in favour of remaining in Canada, rather than staying in a separate Quebec.

Inspired by this, partitionists began to make themselves heard in communities from the Ontario border to Montreal, and beyond to the Eastern townships.

Polls indicated that a majority of anglophones were in favour of some sort of partition, should the OUI side win the next referendum. Nationalists pooh-poohed the idea, but surprisingly, those same polls indicated that 40% of francophones might also favour partition.

The francophone media were startled, perhaps for the first time, by the growing anger and frustration within the anglophone community. The question arose: What do anglos really want?

The governing PQ, anxious for a period of calm after the stormy referendum, took note. In the past, half-hearted attempts by the PQ to attract anglo support had failed miserably. The most visible attempt to woo anglophones came in the early 90s when

AND WHAT DO THESE REJECTED REFERENDUM BALLOTS HAVE IN COMMON?

X Non/No   X Non/No

✓ Non/No   X Non/No

✓ Non/No   ✗ Non/No

A THOUSAND TIMES Non/No   ✓ Non/No

LUCIEN BOUCHARD'S
~~JACQUES PARIZEAU'S~~
~~CAMILLE LAURIN'S~~
~~RENÉ LÉVESQUE'S~~
ONE AND ONLY TOKEN
ANGLO AND "YES" MAN,
DAVID PAYNE...

Jacques Parizeau invited anglo loose-cannon Richard Holden into the separatist fold.

Holden, a self-indulgent former Mulroneyite and member of the Equality Party, was to prove a source of much embarrassment to everyone.

Mind you, there is a handful of long-standing anglo separatists whose convictions date back to the early 70s; none is especially trusted or has much influence in anglophone circles.

The most prominent of these is David Payne, a former priest from England and currently the MNA for Vachon, a predominantly francophone riding.

Payne's advice was sought by Lucien Bouchard in an attempt to throw an olive branch to the anglos. It was decided that Bouchard would give a speech to a select audience in the Centaur Theatre, a bastion of English-language culture in Montreal.

Bouchard's speech was unusually polite and low-key, but was met with a great deal of skepticism, particularly after close examination revealed that he hadn't really said much, even if he said it in a soothing way.

At one point, Bouchard stumbled,

The spirit of the Centaur

revealing a lack of awareness of the anglo community. Referring to popular Gazette columnist Josh Freed, Bouchard called him "Josh Fred."

Maybe he was just nervous in the presence of the enemy. Nevertheless, Bouchard has had little to say to or about anglos ever since. As for David Payne, his role as a champion of anglo rights has been reduced to picking on-air fights with anglo talk show hosts.

The spotlight of "anglo angst" then shone on Howard Galganov, a little-known owner of an ad agency. Galganov would become a brief but bright star.

His first effort was a push to pressure large national companies to display at least some English in their Quebec stores, as is perfectly legal under Bill 101.

Embarrassment is something most national companies like to avoid, and stores such as Eaton, The Bay, Sears, and Radio Shack capitulated to the threat of demonstrations and boycotts.

Galganov's name was suddenly magic. Here, at last, was an anglo who actually got things done!

And then Howard decided to travel to

NEWS ITEM: THE P.Q. WOOS THE ANGLOS...

WHAT IN HELL IS DIJON? GI'ME SOME FRENCH'S MUSTARD, PAL... AND A DIET COKE!

New York for the purpose of informing Wall Street about the nefarious goings-on in Quebec. The PQ was nervous. What if Galganov succeeded?

However, the Galganov trip, which included a jaunt to Washington, quickly turned into a comedy of errors. The American financial community ignored the tour while the Canadian media, in both official languages, wrote it off as a bust.

Undeterred, Galganov then opened a store with the flagrant intention of breaking Quebec's rigid sign laws by

Howard Galganov goes to New York…

exhibiting bilingual signs, with the English and French in equal proportions. The store was ignored by the language police. Howard was not dragged off in chains. The public's, and Howard's, interest in the store fizzled.

And then things got strange.

Galganov began to lash out at the English community itself. He threatened to quit his leadership role following sharp criticism of his efforts by a few radio personalities on CJAD, Montreal's most popular English-language radio station.

He then attacked the Royal Victoria Hospital over its language policies, and called for a large demonstration against the hospital. A small handful of hardline anglos showed up in the falling snow.

Next, Galganov ran as an Independent in the 1997 federal election against Liberal Sheila Finestone in the riding of Mount Royal (Pierre Trudeau's old seat, and one of the safest Liberal seats in the country). Galganov promised to quit politics and leave Quebec if he wasn't elected.

Although Galganov gathered 10,000 votes, more than anyone expected, as of this book's printing, he is looking for a house in Ontario.

...and Washington, D.C.

91

Galganov takes on the Anglos; first radio station CJAD...

...and then the Royal Victoria Hospital

Quebec's Office de la Langue Française was established to promote the French language according to the statutes of Bill 101. The efforts of the OLF swing sharply from the overly zealous to the just plain silly.

In the spring of 1996, OLF language police swooped down on grocery shelves, seizing unilingual tins of gefilte fish, and packages of macaroons and matzoh meal. Jews, who use these imported products during the 8 days of Passover, were enraged.

They weren't alone.

An agreement was reached allowing stores to stock the English-only packages for the 40 days before, during, and for the 20 days after Passover.

And so it goes...

In addition to the caprices of the OLF, anglos have to contend with two prominent PQ cabinet ministers: Deputy Prime Minister Bernard Landry, and Louise Beaudoin, the minister in charge of the OLF.

Although viewed by most francophones as competent ministers, Landry and

April, 1996— Another historic date in the struggle for *Québec*—when *l'Office de la Langue Française* marched on the dreaded unilingual matzoh ball...

Beaudoin are in the habit of regularly pushing anglo hot-buttons. At times this is simply a problem of body language, of intonation – not what they say, so much as how they say it.

Theirs is an arrogance, a contempt for the other, not unlike the attitude of the English towards the French in the hoary old days of Quebec before the Quiet Revolution.

Madame Beaudoin, urging more vigilance on the part of the OLF, hired 15 new "tongue troopers." Soon after, she began to appear in Aislin's Gazette cartoons as a whip-cracking, leather-clad dominatrix. The leather is a perfect fit.

Beaudoin has a particularly shrill manner, commenting about evils of "rampant bilingualism"; she thinks there are too many English services available in hospitals, and she doesn't think Montreal cabbies speak enough French.

So much for the Spirit of the Centaur.

Beaudoin has even mused aloud about the possibility of requiring more French on that final frontier of the free spirit, the Internet; it didn't take much to make her pull in her horns on this one.

DOESN'T OUR RAMPANT LOUISE RESEMBLE THE GRINCH WHO STOLE CHRISTMAS?

Although she likes to appear in steely control of herself at all times, Madame Beaudoin finally blinked and reacted to Aislin's barbs; she stated publicly that the bananas were obviously some sort of sexual reference on the part of the cartoonist. Indeed. But mostly, the banana represents the fleur-de-lys.

Landry's career dates back to the 70s, and the days of René Lévesque. His star has risen steadily in the PQ firmament; at the moment, he is Minister of Finance.

Some are puzzled at how Landry has

TWO FINGERS UP!

GET "DIRTY"

When the Premier of Quebec needs to look good by comparison, who does he get to say really stupid things in his place? He gets Bernie "Dirty" Landry!

WE ASKED THE FINANCE MINISTER, BERNARD LANDRY, WHAT QUÉBEC REALLY WANTS?...

CANADIAN CASH...

survived the cut and thrust of PQ politics over the years. His survival may depend on nothing more than the fact that he knows where all the skeletons are buried.

Like his colleagues, Landry is prone to bumptious, off-the-cuff remarks. He is renowned for a tantrum thrown late on the evening of the Referendum, when an ethnic hotel employee made the mistake of uttering a word of English in his presence.

In spite of the best efforts of Mme Beaudoin and M. Landry to make life unbearable for anglophones, Montreal is, and will always be, a bilingual city.

After some much-needed letting-off of steam, thanks to Howard Galganov, Quebec anglos may now fall back on the middle ground established by the federal and provincial Liberal parties, and the lobby group, Alliance Quebec.

And why not?

After all, there is is this delicious little nugget of irony: Lucien Bouchard has admitted publicly that he speaks mainly English at home with his wife and children.

GUERRILLA?

Mayor of Ville Lasalle accuses partitionists of being guerrillas

Statue of Charles de Gaulle erected in Quebec City

MONTRÉAL

Sketch of Notre Dame de Bonsecours, Old Montreal

Jean Doré, a man of modest talents and matching ambitions, strode into the Mayor's Office in November of 1994, intending to listen to the people – not altogether a bad strategy, given that he succeeded the autocratic Jean Drapeau.

Doré listened, and then proceeded to develop a cumbersome, politically correct, quasi-socialist bureaucracy whose best efforts strangled Montreal with an increasingly complex tangle of rules and regulations. Doré's administration took great pleasure in lavish spending and aggressive taxation; Montreal voters took great pleasure in giving Doré the boot after two terms.

Sadly, voters also threw out the boulevardier with the bathwater; Nick Auf der Mar, Montreal's favourite gadfly and bon vivant, lost his seat after serving 20 years on council.

Auf der Mar, a veteran city columnist for The Gazette, had been under strict orders from the newspaper not to write about municipal politics as long as he was mired

THE LAST OF THE BISHOP STREET MOHICANS...

Nick Auf der Mar defeated

VOTEZ! VOTE, EH?

A suggested all-purpose bilingual election poster

in it. His defeat freed him to take well-aimed pot-shots at the incoming regime.

Pierre Bourque, the new mayor, was a horticulturist by profession; his only political experience had been serving as the president of Jacques Parizeau's riding association for several years.

Bourque was elected on a platform of deregulation, with promises of less talk and more action. Playing to his strength, he also promised to plant a lot of flowers. He tried to speed up the process of government; alas, because of strictures already in place, he was forced to consult the public to see if he would be allowed to consult the public less.

Bourque also tried to prune the municipal payroll, but Montreal's blue-collar workers, overpaid and generally loath to get their hands dirty, simply rolled up their sleeves and worked harder than they ever had before to stop him in his tracks.

Shortly after Bourque's election, rival motorcycle gangs, the Hell's Angels and the Rock Machine, developed a fondness for the car bomb, blowing each other – and the occasional innocent bystander – to smithereens.

Bourque before...

...and Bourque after

Montreal city council has 52 members, more than any other city in North America; Los Angeles, for example, gets by with a mere 15. The councillor's role is questionable anyway, given that the city's executive committee makes most of the decisions. Lately, however, fewer and fewer members of Bourque's Vision Party seem to share his vision – not surprising, considering the recent sale of the city's Blue Bonnets race track to the provincial government for the fire-sale price of $15 million.

Some members of Bourque's party have quit in disgust, and the mayor has been engaged in a long-running, highly embarrassing battle to fire a couple of less-than-loyal members of his executive committee. The future looks grim for Vision Montreal.

To understand Montreal's future, you must look to the past. The city has lost some 300,000 tax-payers over the past 20 years; it is impoverished, ragged and patched, and dependent on the support of the federal and provincial governments.

Rather than help, however, the PQ government is content to dump as many financial responsibilities as it can on Montreal. Off-loading is the reigning

PQ ceremony marks the 30th anniversary of Charles de Gaulle's "Vive le Québec libre!" speech in Montreal

The PQ exerting control over the city of Montreal

And what would Jean Drapeau think of all this?

How to solve the biker wars?

Police caught speeding to pick up French fries

ideology of governments everywhere; it is also a handy way of punishing Montreal, which continues to vote NON.

Recently, the PQ demonstrated its influence in the city by holding a ceremony commemorating the 30th anniversary of the day Charles de Gaulle hurled an intemperate "Vive le Québec libre!" off the balcony of Montreal's city hall. Mayor Bourque ducked out of town just before the event.

On the whole, apart from being able to panhandle in two languages, Montreal's street people are indistinguishable from

Real-life sketch of Montreal city workers

November brings the start of winter

the poor anywhere in North America – no poorer, but certainly colder in winter.

And winter is always with us.

When our city streets are drifted over and there's glare ice on the highways, when the crews are working to rule and refusing any suggestion of overtime (galling, when you consider that in some neighbourhoods, unemployment runs as high as 25%!), Montrealers do the only thing they can – they blame the mayor...and dream of summer festivals.

Although they are really a kind of

December, January...

February, March...

...and April!

Not everyone was invited to Céline Dion's wedding

summer-long urban party for people who can't get away to the cottage, our festivals (jazz, film, comedy) are actually an important source of revenue. Montreal needs all the money it can get given that most of our financial clout has drifted westward. Even the Bank of Montreal has moved most of its offices to Calgary and – shudder! – changed its corporate monicker.

But there are still a few rich people around; now and then one of them deigns to put on a show for the benefit of the little people. Céline Dion, a simple girl from rural Quebec, was recently married in Notre Dame Cathedral; she was swathed in miles of silk, wrapped in yards of costly furs, worshipped by air-conditioned busloads of invited swells, and assisted by more clergy than you could shake a stick at.

In spite of Montreal's problems, the pleasures of living here still outweigh the pain. Unemployment may be high, but Montrealers dine out more than anyone else. And why not? There are thousands of excellent little restos. The political situation may be unstable, but there's an up side to everything: good housing's cheap and plentiful. And the streets are still relatively safe: 1,500,000 people attended the 1997 Jazz Festival, and the

Spring sketches: Old Montreal

police didn't report a single incident. (Many tourists come to politically incorrect Montreal simply to smoke.)

As Anthony Wilson-Smith wrote in Maclean's magazine after a recent visit: "Ninety-nine percent of anglophones and francophones don't argue with each other about language – or anything else."

Montreal – bilingual and bicultural – is also a multi-ethnic collection of people speaking all the languages of the world, living together in joyfully disorganized and chaotic harmony – and if Montreal is to be saved, this is what will save us.

Montreal's casino now open 24 hours a day

Grand Prix driver as lost tourist

Ontario passes tough tobacco bill

TORONTO — Ontario's legislators passed the toughest tobacco-control bill in North America yesterday. The bill makes it illegal for people under the age of 19 to buy cigarettes, and forbids the sale of cigarettes in vending machines and in most health facilities including drug stores. It also further restricts smoking in public areas, including schools, shopping malls and video arcades. The bill also gives the province the right to add health warnings to those required by the federal government and to proceed with so-called plain packaging, although Health Minister Ruth Grier reiterated that she is willing to give Ottawa a chance to act on that issue first.

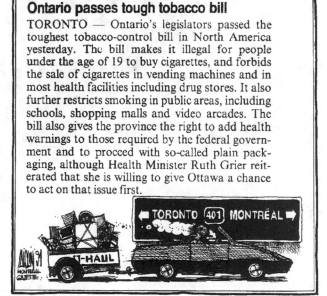

More realistic warning labels on cigarette packs?

Athlete Silken Laumann stripped of Pan-Am gold medal for having taken decongestant Benadryl

Brilliant Expo manager, Felipe Alou

Toe Blake dies

SPORTS

Expo pitcher Pedro Martinez: Spring training, 1996

Although this book is a collection of political observations, there are reasons for including a chapter of sports cartoons: what happens on the playing field often mirrors what's happening in the rest of society; thus, sports cartoons frequently grace the editorial pages of The Gazette.

Montreal's reputation as a sports town took a severe beating in the 90s: our teams stumbled, our stadium crumbled, fans stayed home, prices rose and revenues fell.

Political uncertainty keeps the city poor; people who don't have jobs won't pay good money to watch teams lose. And Montrealers love a winner; we haven't had one lately.

Sadly, we are reminded of past glory only when one of our old heroes falls. Toe Blake died in 1995. Blake played for the Montreal Maroons, and was a mainstay of the Montreal Canadiens "Punch Line," alongside Elmer Lach and the brilliant Rocket Richard.

Blake's teams made winning seem inevitable. A stern and steady coach, his record speaks for itself, and for all time: 8 Stanley Cups between 1955 and 1968.

Montreal's last genuine hockey superstar, Patrick Roy

Patrick Roy traded to Colorado

Red Fisher comments on Stephane Richer being reacquired

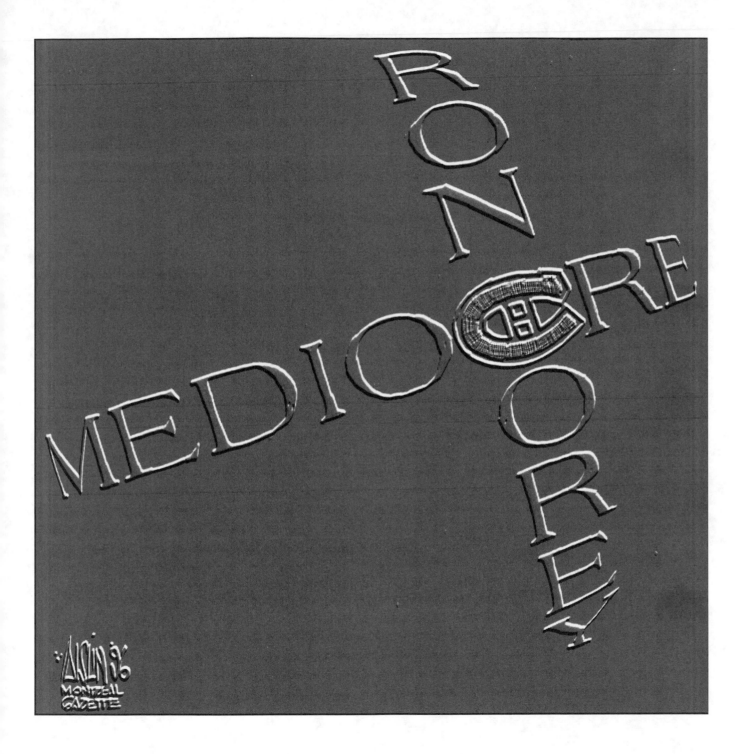

When he died, we were reminded of how far nos glorieux had fallen. The motto of the Canadiens is, "To you with failing hands we throw the torch..." For the past several years, the Habs have managed to find new ways to drop it.

Under the direction of coach Mario Tremblay, the wheels fell off completely: Tremblay and star goalie Patrick Roy had an on-ice spat, and Roy blew up at club president Ron Corey on the way to the dressing room.

Suddenly the best goalie in the league found himself bound for Colorado, of all places, to play for the Avalanche, formerly the Quebec Nordiques. Roy had the last word. He led his new team to the Stanley Cup, and Montreal's humiliation was complete.

Mind you, the team has all the money in the world, more than enough to build a new Forum (suitably named the Molson Centre, suitably nicknamed The Keg).

Hockey purists were surprised by the decision to abandon the Forum, the most famous sports arena in North America; they were embarrassed by the spectacle surrounding the subsequent auction of seats, pennants, and any other saleable item from the building.

Forum fire sale

Own a piece of The Forum forever!

— GENUINE PLASTIC BOX

GENUINE COTTON BATTING

GENUINE WOODEN SPLINTER FROM AN ACTUAL TOILET SEAT IN LES CANADIENS' DRESSING ROOM—A THRONE UPON WHICH ALL THE GREAT LEGENDS SAT!

But Canadiens' management, led by president Ron Corey, continues to be unable to find winning players or a winning formula. The only real consolation – a standard Montreal fall-back in tough times – is that, no matter how bad things are for the Canadiens, things are worse for the Leafs.

At the other end of town, the problems of the Montreal Expos are just the reverse: no

Les Canadiens' only consolation: The Leafs are worse

money but lots of talent; a badly decayed facility, but brilliant on-field leadership.

The Expos were the best team in baseball, and were well on their way to the World Series, when the baseball strike ruined the 1994 and 1995 seasons. After the strike, the cash-strapped Expos had a fire sale – they simply couldn't afford to keep their best players.

Still, year after year, the Expos find a way to cobble together exciting teams from raw, and therefore cheap, talent such as rookies Rondell White and Vladimir Guerrero (widely touted as the next Roberto Clemente).

They also manage to round out the roster with an engaging collection of cast-offs and retreads who somehow blossom under the savvy guidance of Felipe Alou and his coaches.

Left fielder Henry Rodriguez, obtained from the Los Angeles Dodgers, was an instant hit in Montreal, going on a home run spree in 1996. This led to a rare event at the Big O – fan enthusiasm; after each tater, delirious fans threw Oh Henry! chocolate bars onto the field.

Montreal had an important baseball milestone to mark in 1996, and no city

Major League Baseball's strike ends

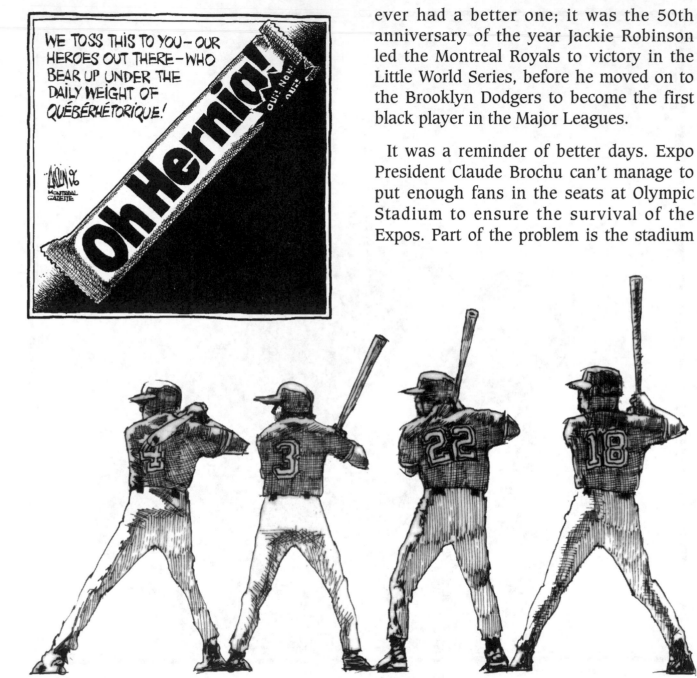

WE TOSS THIS TO YOU – OUR HEROES OUT THERE – WHO BEAR UP UNDER THE DAILY WEIGHT OF QUÉBÉRHÉTORIQUE!

OhHernia!

oui? Non! oui?

ever had a better one; it was the 50th anniversary of the year Jackie Robinson led the Montreal Royals to victory in the Little World Series, before he moved on to the Brooklyn Dodgers to become the first black player in the Major Leagues.

It was a reminder of better days. Expo President Claude Brochu can't manage to put enough fans in the seats at Olympic Stadium to ensure the survival of the Expos. Part of the problem is the stadium

Expo spring training sketchbook – West Palm Beach, Florida, March, 1996

itself; the showpiece of the Montreal Olympics, the Big O was badly built, and it's showing its age. And then there is the location; east-end Montreal simply has no surrounding baseball ambience.

Brochu is proposing that a modest new ballpark be built downtown, at a cost of $250 million; he's convinced location is everything. Downtown worked for Toronto's SkyDome; on the other hand, the ballpark we have still isn't paid for.

If a new stadium is not built, Brochu will sell the team to the highest bidder by 1999 – a devastating blow to the city that sent Jackie Robinson to the majors.

The Expos share Olympic Stadium with the Montreal Alouettes, the storied CFL football franchise that was re-established in 1996. Despite fielding a competitive team, the Als are having even more trouble than the Expos at the box office, and the prospects are not good.

131

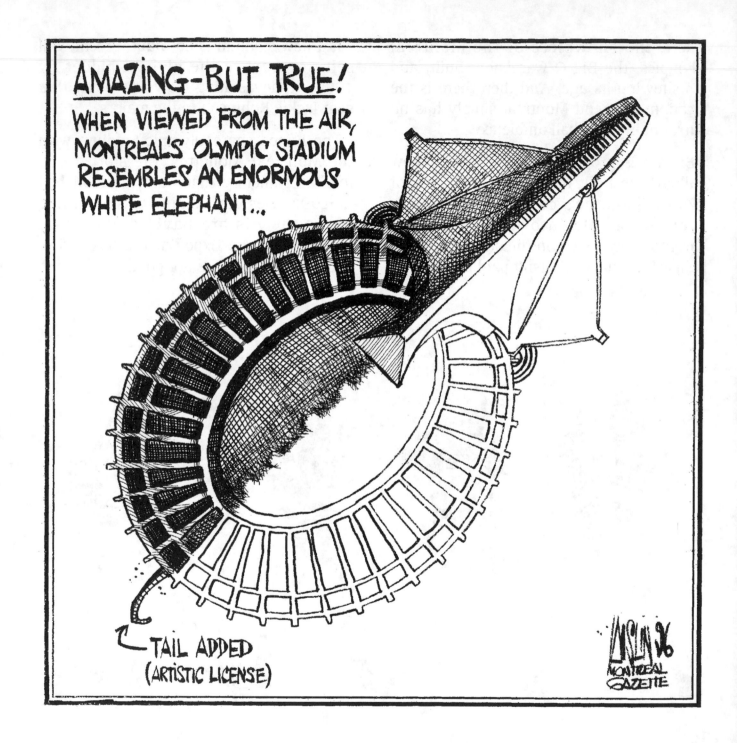

AMAZING-BUT TRUE!
WHEN VIEWED FROM THE AIR, MONTREAL'S OLYMPIC STADIUM RESEMBLES AN ENORMOUS WHITE ELEPHANT...

TAIL ADDED
(ARTISTIC LICENSE)

WHY NOT NAME A STREET AFTER HIM?

50th anniversary of Jackie Robinson playing in Montreal

Football returns to Montreal – but for how long?

Athletes learn to keep their mouths shut in Quebec

More young people are playing football, and Quebec's colleges and universities are turning out plenty of polished players; once again, the problem is both cultural and political: football has always been regarded as an anglo game.

If Montreal were to lose its baseball and its football teams, it would be just another one-horse town; given the present state of Les Canadiens, a faded old dobbin at that.

Political correctness in Quebec means keeping your mouth shut, as former Canadiens star Guy Lafleur found out when he became involved, briefly, in the 1996 Referendum. Lafleur campaigned for the NON side, and was scorched in the French press. He beat a hasty retreat, noting dryly that, "in politics, they play a lot more dirty than in hockey."

Athletes here quickly learn to take no stance or make no statement regarding the politics of language; sometimes, they learn the hard way. In September of 1995, Mike Lansing, the Expos second baseman, said that French seemed hardly necessary over the PA system during a raucous return flight from San Francisco. (The actual second language of the Expos is Spanish.)

Days later, Mike Keane, captain of Les Canadiens, observed that learning French didn't seem necessary, given that the on-ice language of the Habs is English.

Both incidents were pounced on by French-language reporters, and both incidents provoked rabid talk-show ranting for days afterward. Neither athlete has spoken out since; Keane was traded shortly after.

On the international front, Montrealers enjoyed the 1996 Atlanta Games. As you might expect, some people insist on tallying the medals won by Quebec, as opposed to athletes from the rest of Canada. But everyone was appalled by NBC's slanted coverage, which all but ignored Donovan Bailey's brilliant 100-yard dash. For once, we were happy to watch CBC and Radio-Canada.

Rounding out the sports weirdness: in spite of a lot of legal huffing and puffing, there was an exhibition of Extreme Fighting on the Kanawake Reserve.

And then there was the one about West Island resident Greg Rusedski, a tennis player, who travelled to England where he decided to play in the Davis Cup as a Brit rather than as a Canadian.

Canada captures 22 Olympic medals in Atlanta

American coverage of the Olympics

Canadian coverage of the Olympics

Notorious story man, Red Storey

Expo phenom, Vladimir Guerrero – West Palm Beach, Florida, March, 1997

Pointe Claire's Greg Rusedski plays in Davis Cup

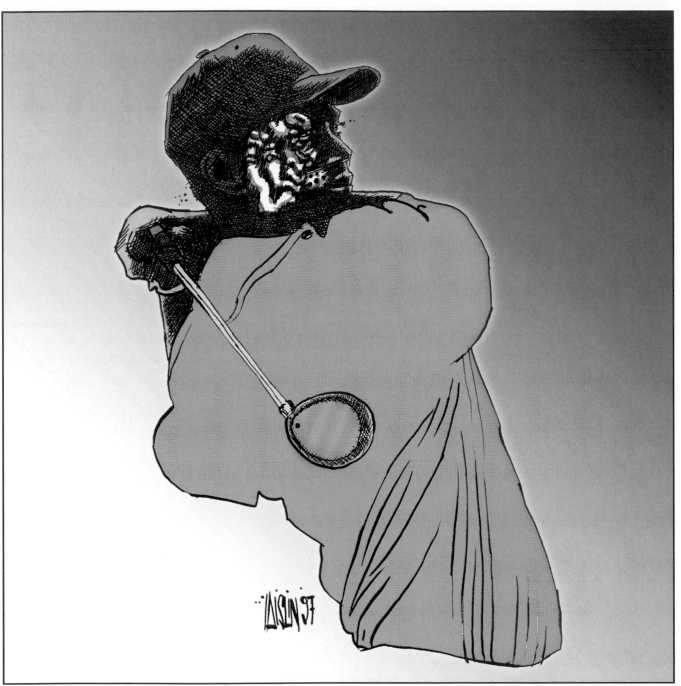

Tiger Woods

Manitoba flood

ELECTION

BUT, SOMETIMES, THEY LET ME OUT TO PLAY

POLLSTER #20

Pollsters are said to be right 19 times out of 20...

On April 27, 1996, Prime Minister Jean Chrétien called an election, to be held on June 2. The 5-week campaign would be the shortest in recent memory. It looked like a cakewalk; to hold onto his majority, all Chrétien would have to do was stay the course and not make any mistakes.

But calling the election when he did was a risk in itself. Southern Manitoba had just been hit with a disastrous flood.

The PM's people sent him west for a photo op. Wearing a bomber jacket and mixing with emergency workers, the PM tossed a token 30-lb. sandbag onto a dike.

Trying to turn the floodwaters into political hay, opposition parties demanded the election be cancelled until the Red River subsided. The Liberals dumped that question in the lap of Chief Electoral Officer Jean-Pierre Kingsley, and continued to campaign. Kingsley ruled that the election should continue.

Preston Manning found a new barber and a new tailor, and had high hopes for Reform. He wanted to knock the Bloc off its perch as Her Majesty's Official Opposition; he did that. He wanted to make a breakthrough in Ontario, crucial if Reform is ever to govern; he didn't do

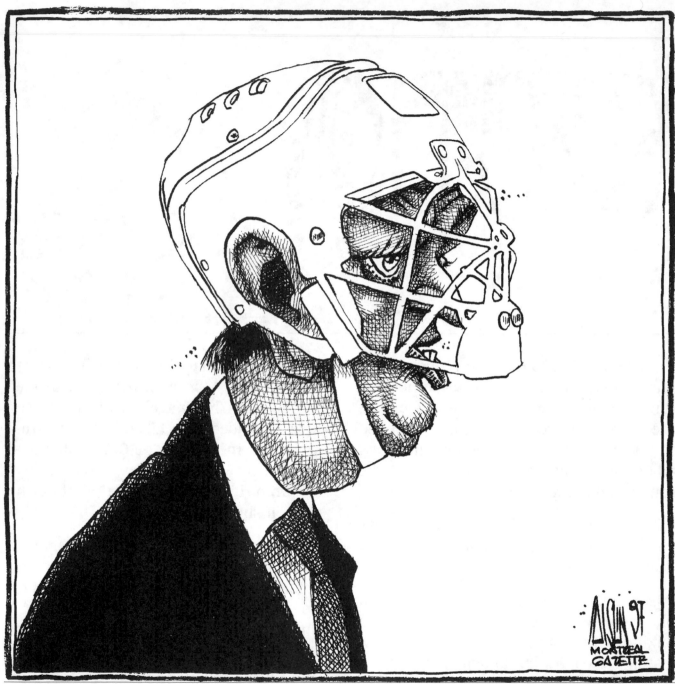

Jean Chrétien calls the election

that. And he wanted to rein in the Tories, who had been gathering momentum under the leadership of bright, bilingual Jean Charest; well, one out of three ain't bad.

Charest shone in the English- and French-language debates. Chrétien did well to hold his own. Manning, thankfully, used a translator in the French debate.

Charest would have to scratch and claw to get the Tories back on the electoral map, having been reduced to 2 seats thanks to the incompetent leadership of Kim Campbell. He started in a hurry – everyone likes Charest.

He has what it takes to be Prime Minister and he's a strong federalist, one of the few Quebeckers who rivals Lucien Bouchard in popularity. But people began to ask, "Where's the rest of the talent?" The best Charest could do was recruit retired Major-General Lewis Mackenzie; Mackenzie lost in Parry Sound-Muskoka.

Alexa McDonough had an uphill battle to regain Official Party status for the NDP. She provided some stirring left-wing rhetoric and promised pie in the sky, which she could well afford to do, given that there wasn't a hope in hell of the NDP forming the government.

Gilles Duceppe visits a cheese factory

The Bloc simply wanted to hang on to what it had, but they started the campaign in disarray. Lucien Bouchard's replacement, Michel Gauthier, was pushed aside smartly by Bouchard's old henchman, Gilles Duceppe.

Duceppe ran an error-prone campaign, the low point of which will be remembered forever: visiting a cheese factory in rural Quebec, he donned a protective shower cap. The subsequent silly photos showed up on the front page of every daily paper the next day – and in every editorial cartoon the day after that.

Bloc supporters are primarily rural, unilingual and anti-English, just as Reform supporters are largely rural, unilingual and, if not anti-French, then certainly anti-Quebec. In fact, there isn't much difference between the two mentalities. But Reform made a big error, running an anti-Quebec ad which cost them votes, seeming to confirm eastern fears that Reform is racist at its core.

Election night began with a bang in the Maritimes, where Tory and NDP members made great gains. But the centre of the country held firm, and – despite Reform's strong showing in the west – the Liberals hung on to a bare majority.

ELECTION BESTIARY

ALMOST EXTINCT, THE DODO BIRD IS ABOUT THE SAME SIZE AS A TURKEY. WITH ITS USELESS WINGS AND TAIL FEATHERS, THE DODO IS UNABLE TO FLY, KEEPING IT MIRED DOWN ON THE GROUND AROUND 10%...

PREDICTABLE LEFTIST RHETORIC

ELECTION BESTIARY

NOW HERE'S A DEPRESSING THOUGHT: THIS COLLECTION OF STUBBORN, ARROGANT JACKASSES IS THE ONE AND ONLY GROUP EVEN REMOTELY CAPABLE OF ACTUALLY GOVERNING THIS COUNTRY

The NDP and the Tories reestablished themselves as Official Parties, but it will be a long while before they become serious players. Reform took over as Official Opposition from the Bloc, but, at the moment, the Liberals are the only "national party" capable of governing.

Jean Charest should have some important role to play in the country's future; whether he will make that contribution as leader of the Tories remains to be seen.

In case anyone had doubts, the election proved that Gilles Duceppe was no Bouchard; the Bloc held onto 44 seats in Quebec, but 60% of Quebeckers voted for federalist parties. Bouchard blustered that this was the last time Quebeckers would vote in a federal election; whatever happens, the smart money says there won't be a Duceppe to vote for.

Preston Manning vowed that, if he were Leader of the Opposition, he would not move into Stornoway; the official residence was too grand and too expensive for a Reformer. But apparently, thousands of Canadians demanded he move in (we were never shown the letters or the faxes), and Preston, without a blush, bowed to popular demand; he'll be moving in as soon as the $68,000 renovation is complete.

Reform makes strategic error in running anti-Quebec ad

Jean Chrétien on election night?

After the election Canadians were clearly tired of politics. The Queen came to Newfoundland for the 500th anniversary of John Cabot's arrival, although where Cabot really arrived is anybody's guess. The Queen and Prince Philip then pushed on to Ontario and the west, prudently skipping Quebec, comme d'habitude.

As for the rest of us, we're taking it easy for the rest of the summer of 1997, relieved that there are no more elections or referendums on the immediate horizon.

That's not to say the nonsense will stop, of course.

What can we expect between now and the millennium?

More of the same.

There will be another Quebec election at some point; even if the PQ wins, there won't be a referendum unless they're sure they can win it. And so Quebec will continue to make noises about separation – but won't. Lucien Bouchard will be humiliated by Canada 478 times, and his government will continue to yank Montreal's chain, bitter about the continued loss of support for separation in the only city that really matters in Quebec.

Never mind through July...

…and August

Montrealers in the meantime will fret about their city and its ongoing loss of its image as a North American metropolis. (Could it be that Milwaukee will be able to hold onto a major league baseball franchise while Montreal won't?)

Our problems seem minuscule in comparison to trouble spots around the world like Belfast or the Middle East.

So why can't we resolve them?

As residents of what the UN calls the best country in the world, we continue to put up with the political horseplay as Canada and Quebec – CanBec – go round and round, with one oar in the water…

ENDLESS, RECYCLED CONVERSATIONS...

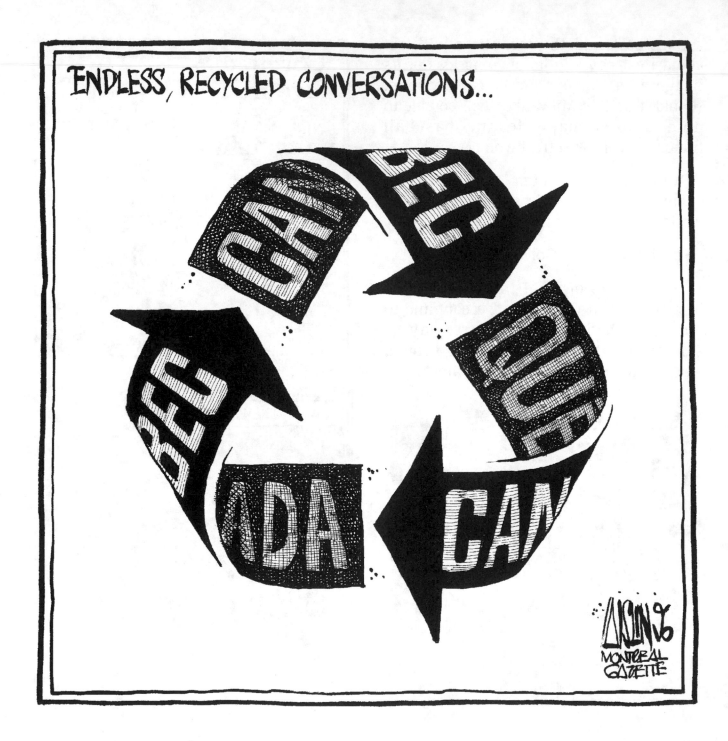

The Queen visits Canada, hop-scotching over Quebec